# Thank you...

...for purchasing this copy of Spelling for Literacy for ages 5-7. We hope that you will find these 178 worksheets helpful as part of your programme of literacy activities.

Please note that photocopies can only be made for use by the purchasing institution; supplying copies to other schools, institutions or individuals breaches the copyright licence. Thank you for your help in this.

This Spelling for Literacy book is part of our growing range of educational titles. Most of our books are individual workbooks but, due to popular demand, we are now introducing a greater number of photocopiable titles especially for teachers. You may like to look out for:

**HOMEWORK TODAY** for ages 9-10

**HOMEWORK TODAY** for ages 10-11

**NUMERACY TODAY** for ages 5-7

**NUMERACY TODAY** for ages 7-9

**NUMERACY TODAY** for ages 9-11

**SPELLING FOR LITERACY** For ages 7-8

**SPELLING FOR LITERACY** For ages 8-9

**SPELLING FOR LITERACY** For ages 9-10

**SPELLING FOR LITERACY** For ages 10-11

**BEST HANDWRITING** for ages 7-11

To find details of our other publications, please visit our website: **www.acblack.com**

Andrew Brodie Publications

# Suggestions for using this book...

We have examined carefully the current national policies for teaching spelling as part of your literacy work. In writing this book we have included words and spelling patterns which are specified within these policies. We have arranged the words into sets, usually of ten words but in some cases twelve. Each set of words is used in three styles of sheet:

## Sheet A

✓ Can be photocopied onto OHP transparencies for discussion.

✓ Can be displayed on the wall as 'Words of the Week'.

✓ Can be copied onto card and cut up to make matching cards.

## Sheet B

✓ Activity sheets to be used in the Literacy Hour.

✓ A perfect follow-up activity for the learning which has taken place using sheet A.

✓ Often includes a drawing activity.

## Sheet C

✓ Has a fold line so that children can copy the words, then cover them to write again without looking.

✓ Can be hole-punched to go in pupils' personal spelling files.

✓ Can be given as homework sheets.

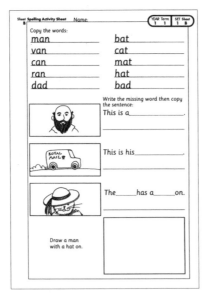

# Spelling for Literacy *for ages 5-7*

## Contents

| | | |
|---|---|---|
| Set 1<br>Sheets A, B & C | Year 1<br>Term 1 | man, van, can, ran, bat, cat, mat, hat, dad, bad |
| Set 2<br>Sheets A, B & C | Year 1<br>Term 1 | sad, bag, had, has, gas, wax, wag, tap, gap, lap |
| Set 3<br>Sheets A, B & C | Year 1<br>Term 1 | web, bed, get, ten, net, leg, red, men, wet, yes |
| Set 4<br>Sheets A, B & C | Year 1<br>Term 1 | pig, dig, did, if, bin, sit, six, his, him, it |
| Set 5<br>Sheets A, B & C | Year 1<br>Term 1 | hot, top, got, pot, hop, fox, dog, dot, not, job |
| Set 6<br>Sheets A, B & C | Year 1<br>Term 1 | cup, bug, mum, put, hug, mud, run, cut, but, us |
| Set 7<br>Sheets A, B & C | Year 1<br>Term 2 | sack, lock, neck, pick, sock, duck, back, lick, luck, peck |
| Set 8<br>Sheets A, B & C | Year 1<br>Term 2 | muff, kiss, huff, toss, mess, puff, off, miss, less, fuss |
| Set 9<br>Sheets A, B & C | Year 1<br>Term 2 | ball, tall, all, tell, hill, pull, hall, bell, will, call |
| Set 10<br>Sheets A, B & C | Year 1<br>Term 2 | sing, king, song, hung, ring, wing, long, bang, rung, hang |
| Set 11<br>Sheets A, B & C | Year 1<br>Term 2 | black, blush, blot, blast, blow, brick, brush, brown, brother, bring |
| Set 12<br>Sheets A, B & C | Year 1<br>Term 2 | crab, crack, crust, dry, crib, drip, drum, dress, drop, cross |
| Set 13<br>Sheets A, B & C | Year 1<br>Term 2 | flag, frog, flip, flop, frill, fry, frost, flat, from, fling |
| Set 14<br>Sheets A, B & C | Year 1<br>Term 2 | glass, glue, glad, glide, grin, grow, grill, glow, grab, grip |
| Set 15<br>Sheets A, B & C | Year 1<br>Term 2 | pram, pray, prick, prod, plum, plant, plan, press, plot, play |
| Set 16<br>Sheets A, B & C | Year 1<br>Term 2 | scar, scarf, scrap, screen, screw, scales, scrub, scooter, scab, scruffy |
| Set 17<br>Sheets A, B & C | Year 1<br>Term 2 | skip, ski, skin, slab, skirt, sleep, slug, skates, skid, slip |
| Set 18<br>Sheets A, B & C | Year 1<br>Term 2 | spade, smell, snap, spot, smile, snow, spider, spoon, small, sniff |
| Set 19<br>Sheets A, B & C | Year 1<br>Term 2 | splash, spring, split, squash, swim, swing, square, spray, spread, squeeze |

| | | |
|---|---|---|
| Set 20<br>Sheets A, B & C | Year 1<br>Term 2 | tree, train, trot, twin, twig, twenty, tractor, twist, trip, trap |
| Set 21<br>Sheets A, B & C | Year 1<br>Term 2 | three, throat, this, they, throw, shoe, shirt, ship, shop, she |
| Set 22<br>Sheets A, B & C | Year 1<br>Term 2 | there, where, them, that, what, chair, chin, church, when, there |
| Set 23<br>Sheets A, B & C | Year 1<br>Term 2 | cold, gold, wild, child, belt, bolt, melt, old, felt, help |
| Set 24<br>Sheets A, B & C | Year 1<br>Term 2 | hand, sand, kind, find, pond, milk, calf, half, and, next |
| Set 25<br>Sheets A, B & C | Year 1<br>Term 2 | camp, lamp, jump, thank, stamp, pink, drink, act, fact, think |
| Set 26<br>Sheets A, B & C | Year 1<br>Term 2 | left, lift, lunch, bunch, mask, branch, bench, filth, ask, crunch |
| Set 27<br>Sheets A, B & C | Year 1<br>Term 2 | vest, dust, kept, must, post, list, last, best, most, fast, just |
| Set 28<br>Sheets A, B & C | Year 1 Term 3 &<br>Year 2 Term 1 | sweet, tea, been, asleep, sea, leaf, seat, read, seen, street |
| Set 29<br>Sheets A, B & C | Year 1 Term 3 &<br>Year 2 Term 1 | rain, name, came, again, day, take, make, away, may, made |
| Set 30<br>Sheets A, B & C | Year 1 Term 3 &<br>Year 2 Term 1 | pie, tie, nice, time, mice, night, bike, fly, try, by |
| Set 31<br>Sheets A, B & C | Year 1 Term 3 &<br>Year 2 Term 1 | coat, boat, home, hope, rose, toes, coach, hose, goes, toe |
| Set 32<br>Sheets A, B & C | Year 1 Term 3 &<br>Year 2 Term 1 | boot, school, too, soon, tooth, blue, room, new, grew, June |
| Set 33<br>Sheets A, B & C | Year 1 Term 3 &<br>Year 2 Term 1 | an, as, can, can't, do, don't, is, isn't, be, because, him, night, or, so, want, said |
| Set 34<br>Sheets A, B & C | Year 1 Term 3 &<br>Year 2 Term 1 | one, two, three, four, five, six, seven, eight, nine, ten |
| Set 35<br>Sheets A, B & C | Year 2<br>Term 1 | look, book, cook, took, foot, wood, hood, cooking, stood, looking |
| Set 36<br>Sheets A, B & C | Year 2<br>Term 1 | car, card, carpet, farmer, star, farm, shark, garden, sharp, market |
| Set 37<br>Sheets A, B & C | Year 2<br>Term 1 | boy, toy, enjoy, annoy, royal, oil, coin, noisy, voice, noise |
| Set 38<br>Sheets A, B & C | Year 2<br>Term 1 | owl, town, how, down, frown, crown, shower, flower, now, crowd |
| Set 39<br>Sheets A, B & C | Year 2<br>Term 1 | mouse, house, out, about, shout, pound, mouth, count, loud, thousand |

| Set 40 Sheets A, B & C | Year 2 Term 1 | Monday, Tuesday, Wednesday, Thursday, Friday, Saturday, Sunday, today |
|---|---|---|
| Set 41 Sheets A, B & C | Year 2 Term 1 | you, they, get, after, going, push, over, went, getting, are |
| Set 42 Sheets A, B & C | Year 2 Term 2 | fair, hair, pair, air, repair, chair, stairs, fairy, there, where |
| Set 43 Sheets A, B & C | Year 2 Term 2 | pear, bear, wear, their, tear, stare, scare, care, share, square |
| Set 44 Sheets A, B & C | Year 2 Term 2 | fork, horse, born, sport, morning, forty, door, story, floor, poor |
| Set 45 Sheets A, B & C | Year 2 Term 2 | saw, claw, yawn, dawn, autumn, sauce, paw, caught, taught, crawl |
| Set 46 Sheets A, B & C | Year 2 Term 2 | core, snore, more, store, explore, sore, tore, bored, before, wore |
| Set 47 Sheets A, B & C | Year 2 Term 2 | bigger, brother, her, were, over, under, sister, water, other, another |
| Set 48 Sheets A, B & C | Year 2 Term 2 | bird, girl, first, third, circle, stir, dirty, thirty, thirsty, thirteen |
| Set 49 Sheets A, B & C | Year 2 Term 2 | fur, curl, curve, purpose, nurse, burn, curtains, hurt, return, surprise |
| Set 50 Sheets A, B & C | Year 2 Term 3 | ear, hear, near, clear, tear, beard, fear, disappear, appear, dear |
| Set 51 Sheets A, B & C | Year 2 Term 3 | head, bread, instead, tread, spread, feather, heavy, weather, ready, steady |
| Set 52 Sheets A, B & C | Year 2 Term 3 | eleven, twelve, thirteen, fourteen, fifteen, sixteen, seventeen, eighteen, nineteen, twenty |
| Set 53 Sheets A, B & C | Year 2 Term 3 | red, orange, yellow, green, blue, purple, pink, brown, black, white |
| Set 54 Sheets A, B & C | Year 2 Term 3 | laugh, little, some, went, come, called, with, could, should, have, would, here |
| Set 55 Sheets A, B & C | Year 2 Term 3 | love, people, lived, many, who, live, much, very, our, than, your, once |
| Set 56 Sheets A, B & C | Year 2 Term 3 | January, February, March, April, May, June, July, August, September, October, November, December |

● **Short vowel sounds**

man

van

can        ran

bat

cat

mat

hat

dad        bad

For use
with OHP,
for display
or
to make
matching
cards.

Copy the words:

man _____        bat _____
van _____        cat _____
can _____        mat _____
ran _____        hat _____
dad _____        bad _____

Write the missing word, then copy the sentence:

This is a_____.

_____

This is his_____.

_____

The_____has a_____on.

_____

Draw a man
with a hat on.

Yr1 week 3    3.12.06

**LEARN, WRITE, CHECK.**
● **Short vowel sounds**

Name: _ _ _ _ _ _ _ _ _ _ _ _ _ _

| Learn the word | Write then cover | Write then check |
|---|---|---|
| man | | |
| van | | |
| can | | |
| ran | | |
| bat | | |
| cat | | |
| mat | | |
| hat | | |
| dad | | |
| bad | | |

*Fold-line*

Sheet
A

● **Short vowel sounds**

YEAR
**1**
Term
**1**

SET
**2**
Sheet
A

For use
with OHP,
for display
or
to make
matching
cards.

| | |
|---|---|
| sad | |
| bag | |
| had | has |
| gas | |
| wax | |
| wag | |
| tap | |
| gap | lap |

LAR-

Copy the words:

sad _____    wag _____
had _____    bag _____
has _____    tap _____
gas _____    gap _____
wax _____    lap _____

Choose one of these words to fill the gap, then copy the sentence:

This girl is_____.

_____

The dog can_____its tail.

_____

_____

The_____has a drip.

_____

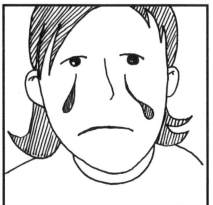

This girl is sad.

Draw a happy girl or boy.

Name: _____   **LEARN, WRITE, CHECK.**
                        ● **Short vowel sounds**

| YEAR | Term | SET | Sheet |
|------|------|-----|-------|
| 1    | 1    | 2   | C     |

| Learn the word | Write then cover | Write then check |
|----------------|------------------|------------------|
| sad | | |
| bag | | |
| had | | |
| has | | |
| gas | | |
| wax | | |
| wag | | |
| tap | | |
| gap | | |
| lap | | |

*Fold-line*

Year 1 - Week 2

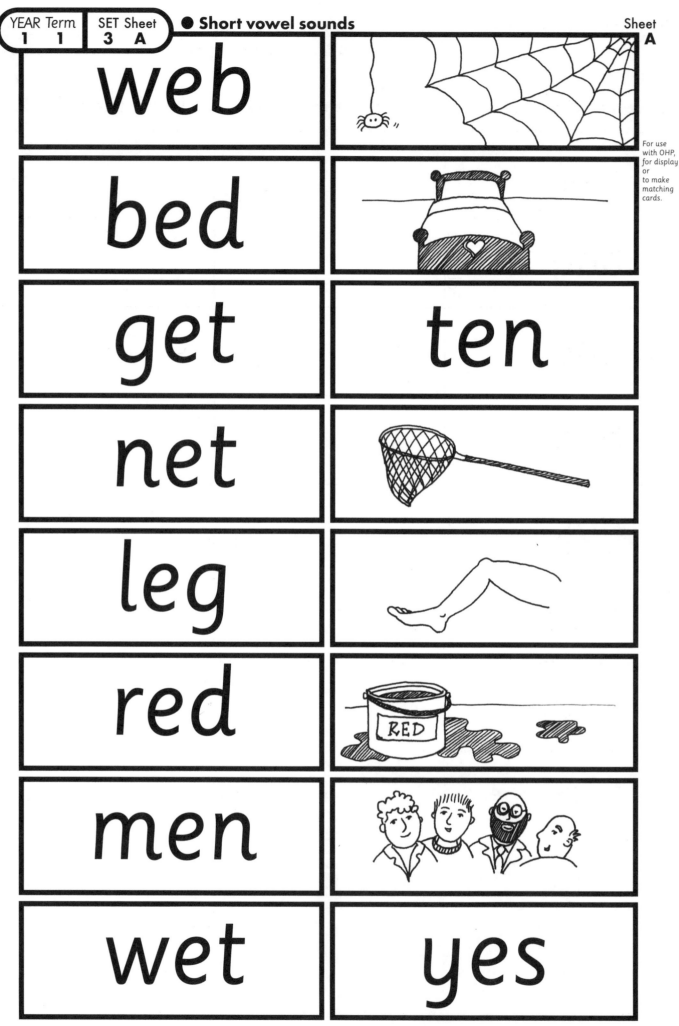

web

bed

get

net

leg

red

men

wet

ten

yes

For use with OHP, for display or to make matching cards.

Copy the words:

web _____    leg _____

wet _____    bed _____

get _____    red _____

net _____    ten _____

yes _____    men _____

Write the missing words,
then copy the sentence:

Here are _____ _____.

_____

The boy is in _____.

_____

The_____is_____.

_____

Draw a red hat.

This is a _____ hat.

18.12.06

**LEARN, WRITE, CHECK.**
● **Short vowel sounds**

Name: _ _ _ _ _ _ _ _ _ _ _ _

| Learn the word | Write then cover | Write then check |
|---|---|---|
| web   1, | | |
| bed   2.   Fold-line | | |
| get   3 | | |
| ten   4 | | |
| net   5 | | |
| leg   6 | | |
| red   7 | | |
| men   8 | | |
| wet   9 | | |
| yes   10 | | |

● **Short vowel sounds**

For use
with OHP,
for display
or
to make
matching
cards.

pig

dig

did

if

bin

sit

six

**6**

his

hers

him

it

Copy the words:

pig _____    if _____

dig _____    it _____

did _____    sit _____

his _____    six _____

him _____    bin _____

Write the missing word,
then copy the sentence:

This is a big _____.

_____

This is a _____.

_____

Draw six bins. Colour them red.

Here are _____ red _____.

Name: _____

**LEARN, WRITE, CHECK.**
● **Short vowel sounds**

YEAR Term 1 1 — SET Sheet 4 C

S.10.07

| Learn the word | Write then cover | Write then check |
|---|---|---|
| pig | | |
| dig | | |
| did | | |
| if | | |
| bin | | |
| sit | | |
| six | | |
| his | | |
| him | | |
| it | | |

Fold-line

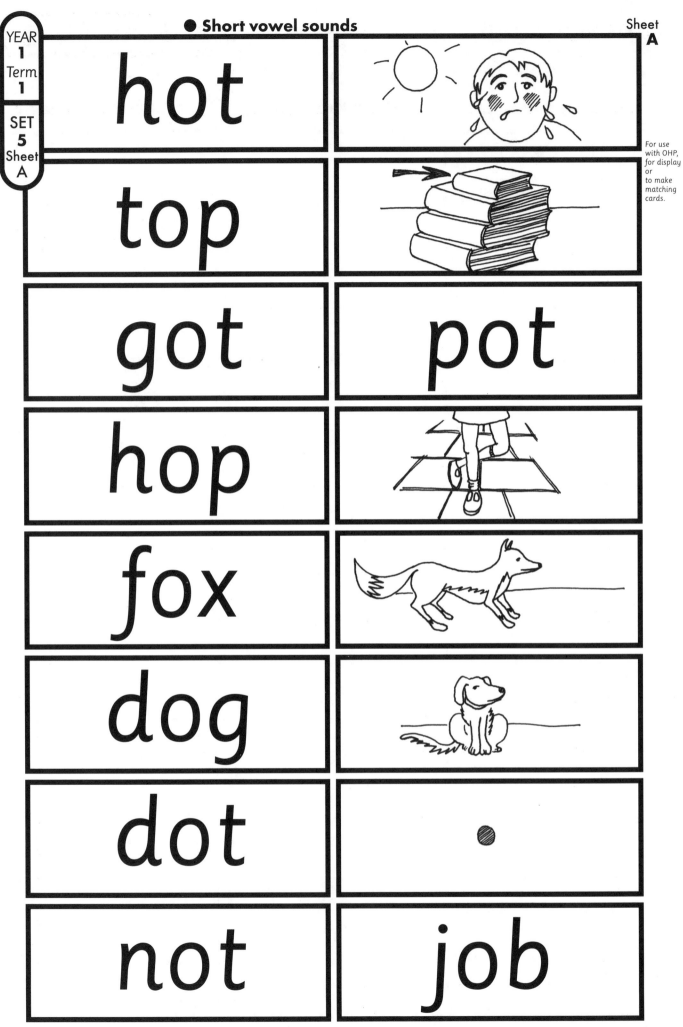

hot

top

got

pot

hop

fox

dog

dot

not

job

For use
with OHP,
for display
or
to make
matching
cards.

Copy the words:

hot _____          top _____

not _____          hop _____

got _____          job _____

dot _____          dog _____

pot _____          fox _____

Write the missing words,
then copy the sentence:

The _____ is _____.

_____

The_____ is at the_____ .

_____

Draw a big dog.
Write about your picture.

_____

_____

_____

_____

_____

| YEAR Term | SET Sheet | | |
|:---:|:---:|---|---|
| 1  1 | 5  C | **LEARN, WRITE, CHECK.** | Name: _____ |
| | | ● **Short vowel sounds** | |

| Learn the word | Write then cover | Write then check |
|---|---|---|
| hot | | |
| top | | |
| got | | |
| pot | | |
| hop | | |
| fox | | |
| dog | | |
| dot | | |
| not | | |
| job | | |

*Fold-line*

● **Short vowel sounds**

For use
with OHP,
for display
or
to make
matching
cards.

| cup | |
| bug | |
| mum | put |
| hug | |
| mud | |
| run | |
| cut | |
| but | us |

Name: _ _ _ _ _ _ _ _ _ _ _

Copy the words:

cup _____     hug _____

cut _____     bug _____

but _____     run _____

put _____     mum _____

us _____      mud _____

Write the missing word, then copy the sentence:

The boots have_____on them.

_____

_____

Draw three cups.

Here are three _____ .

_____

Draw two bugs.

Here is a bug.

Name: _____

**LEARN, WRITE, CHECK.**
● **Short vowel sounds**

YEAR Term 1 1 | SET Sheet 6 C

| Learn the word | Write then cover | Write then check |
|---|---|---|
| cup | | |
| bug | | |
| mum | | |
| put | | |
| hug | | |
| mud | | |
| run | | |
| cut | | |
| but | | |
| us | | |

Fold-line

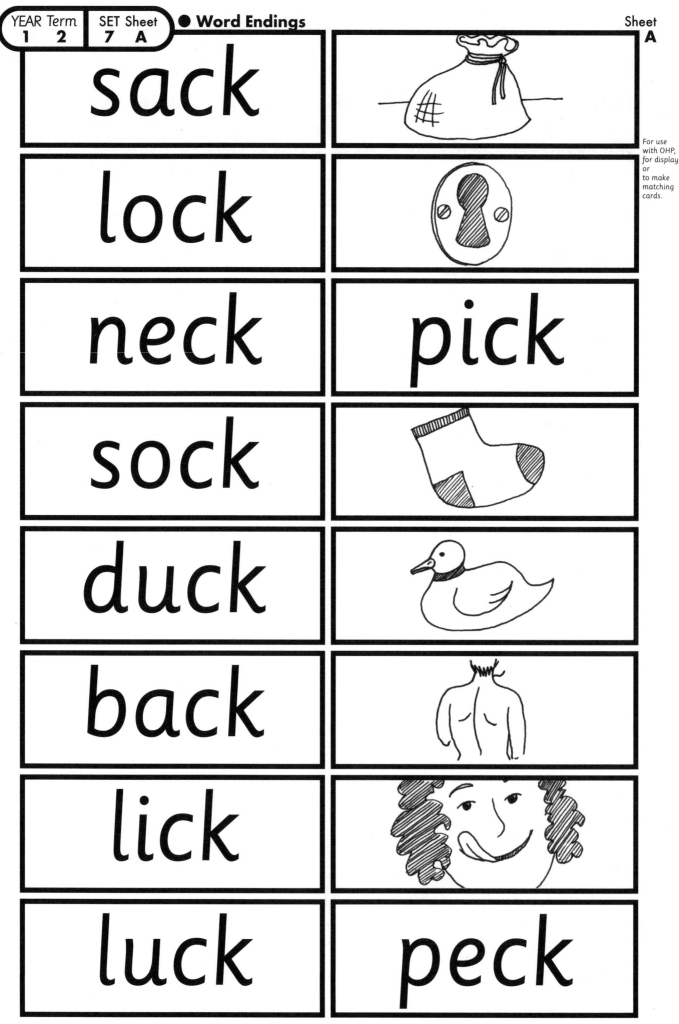

YEAR Term
1  2

SET Sheet
7  A

● **Word Endings**

**Sheet A**

For use
with OHP,
for display
or
to make
matching
cards.

sack

lock

neck

pick

sock

duck

back

lick

luck

peck

© Andrew Brodie Publications ✓ www.acblack.com

Copy the words:

| | |
|---|---|
| sack | lick |
| back | pick |
| sock | peck |
| lock | neck |
| luck | duck |

Write the word for each picture.

Write about the picture.

_____
_____
_____
_____

| YEAR Term 1 2 | SET Sheet 7 C | LEARN, WRITE, CHECK. |
| --- | --- | --- |

**● Word Endings**

Name: _ _ _ _ _ _ _ _ _ _ _ _

| Learn the word | Write then cover | Write then check |
| --- | --- | --- |
| sack | | |
| lock | | |
| neck | | |
| pick | | |
| sock | | |
| duck | | |
| back | | |
| lick | | |
| luck | | |
| peck | | |

Fold-line

Sheet
**A**

● **Word Endings**

YEAR
**1**
Term
**2**

SET
**8**
Sheet
**A**

For use
with OHP,
for display
or
to make
matching
cards.

| muff | |
| kiss | |
| huff | toss |
| mess | |
| puff | |
| off | |
| miss | |
| less | fuss |

Copy the words:

off                          mess

muff                         miss

huff                         kiss

puff                         fuss

less                         toss

Write the word for each picture.

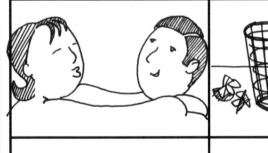   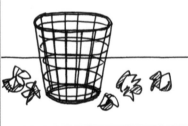   

Fill in the missing words in this sentence:

The wolf said, "With a _____ and a _____ I will blow your house down."

Name: _____   **LEARN, WRITE, CHECK.**
● **Word Endings**

| Learn the word | Write then cover | Write then check |
|---|---|---|
| muff | | |
| kiss | | |
| huff | | |
| toss | | |
| mess | | |
| puff | | |
| off | | |
| miss | | |
| less | | |
| fuss | | |

Fold-line

● **Word Endings**

Sheet
**A**

YEAR
**1**
Term
**2**

SET
**9**
Sheet
A

For use
with OHP,
for display
or
to make
matching
cards.

| | |
|---|---|
| ball | |
| tall | |
| all | tell |
| hill | |
| pull | |
| hall | |
| bell | |
| will | call |

Copy the words:

| | |
|---|---|
| all | hill |
| ball | will |
| call | bell |
| tall | tell |
| hall | pull |

Draw a picture for each word.

| | | |
|---|---|---|
| | | |
| hill | bell | ball |

Write the word for each picture.

Write about the picture.

_____

_____

_____

_____

20.11.06

**LEARN, WRITE, CHECK.**
● **Word Endings**

Name: _ _ _ _ _ _ _ _ _ _ _ _

| Learn the word | Write then cover | Write then check |
|---|---|---|
| ball | | |
| tall | | |
| all | | |
| tell | | |
| hill | | |
| pull | | |
| hall | | |
| bell | | |
| will | | |
| call | | |

Fold-line

For use
with OHP,
for display
or
to make
matching
cards.

● **Word Endings**

| sing | |
| king | |
| song | hung |
| ring | |
| wing | |
| long | |
| bang | |
| rung | hang |

Copy the words:

wing            long

ring            rung

king            hung

sing            hang

song            bang

Write the missing word, then copy the sentence:

The gun made a loud

_____ .

_____

_____

Draw a king wearing a ring.

Write about the picture.

_____

_____

_____

_____

_____

_____

_____

_____

Name: _____    **LEARN, WRITE, CHECK.**
                           ● **Word Endings**

| YEAR Term | SET Sheet |
|-----------|-----------|
| 1    2    | 10   C    |

| Learn the word | Write then cover | Write then check |
|----------------|------------------|------------------|
| sing | | |
| king | | |
| song | | |
| hung | | |
| ring | | |
| wing | | |
| long | | |
| bang | | |
| rung | | |
| hang | | |

Fold-line

YEAR
**1**
Term
**2**

SET
**11**
Sheet
A

black

blush

blot

blast

blow

brick

brush

brown

brother

bring

For use
with OHP,
for display
or
to make
matching
cards.

Copy the words:

black                    brick

blast                    bring

blot                     brown

blow                     brother

blush                    brush

Write the missing word, then copy
the sentence:

This square is _____.

_____

I can _____ the candles
out.

_____

_____

This is a _____ wall.

_____

Draw a house made of bricks.
Write about the house.

_____

_____

_____

1.12.06

**LEARN, WRITE, CHECK.**
● **Initial Consonant Clusters**

Name: _ _ _ _ _ _ _ _ _ _ _ _

| Learn the word | Write then cover | Write then check |
|---|---|---|
| black | | |
| blush | | |
| blot | | |
| blast | | |
| blow | | |
| brick | | |
| brush | | |
| brown | | |
| brother | | |
| bring | | |

Fold-line

Sheet
**A**

● **Initial Consonant Clusters**

YEAR
**1**
Term
**2**

SET
**12**
Sheet
**A**

For use
with OHP,
for display
or
to make
matching
cards.

crab

crack

crust

dry

crib

drip

drum

dress

drop

cross

Name: _ _ _ _ _ _ _ _ _ _ _ _

Copy the words:

crib_____     dry_____

crab_____     drip_____

crack_____     drop_____

cross_____     dress_____

crust_____     drum_____

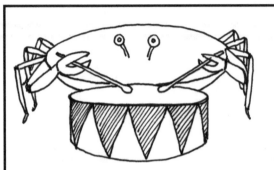

Write the missing word, then copy the sentence:

The _____ is playing
the _____.

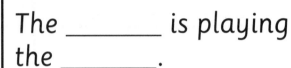

_____

_____

Draw six girls with different colour dresses.

Draw six boys with different colour shorts.

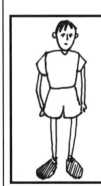

3.12.06

Name: _ _ _ _ _ _ _ _ _ _ _ _     **LEARN, WRITE, CHECK.**
● **Initial Consonant Clusters**

| Learn the word | Write then cover | Write then check |
|---|---|---|
| crab | | |
| crack | | |
| crust | | |
| dry | | |
| crib | | |
| drip | | |
| drum | | |
| dress | | |
| drop | | |
| cross | | |

Fold-line

YEAR
1
Term
2

SET
13
Sheet
A

For use with OHP, for display or to make matching cards.

flag

frog

flip

flop

frill

fry

frost

flat

from

fling

Copy the words:

flag _____    frog _____

flat _____    from _____

fling _____    fry _____

flip _____    frill _____

flop _____    frost _____

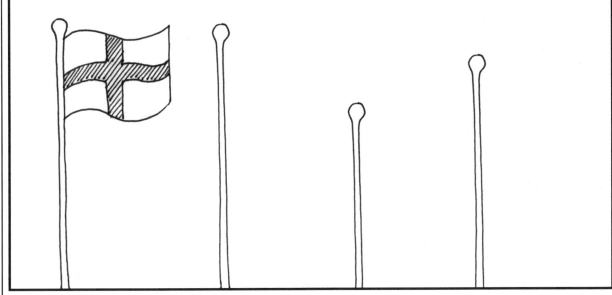

Write the missing word, then copy the sentence:

The _____is flying on the flats.

_____

_____

Draw three more flags. Colour each flag.

**YEAR Term** 1 2 | **SET Sheet** 13 C

**LEARN, WRITE, CHECK.**
● **Initial Consonant Clusters**

Name: _ _ _ _ _ _ _ _ _ _

| Learn the word | Write then cover | Write then check |
|---|---|---|
| flag | | |
| frog | | |
| flip | | |
| flop | | |
| frill | | |
| fry | | |
| frost | | |
| flat | | |
| from | | |
| fling | | |

*Fold-line*

● **Initial Consonant Clusters**

For use
with OHP,
for display
or
to make
matching
cards.

| | |
|---|---|
| glass | |
| glue | |
| glad | glide |
| grin | |
| grow | |
| grill | |
| glow | |
| grab | grip |

Name: _ _ _ _ _ _ _ _ _ _

Copy the words:

glad

glass

glide

glow

glue

grab

grin

grip

grill

grow

The plant will _____ if we give it some water.

_____

_____

This plane can _____.

_____

Draw a man with a grin.

Write about the picture.

_____

_____

_____

_____

20.12.06

Name: _____  **LEARN, WRITE, CHECK.**
● **Initial Consonant Clusters**

| Learn the word | Write then cover | Write then check |
| --- | --- | --- |
| glass | | |
| glue | | |
| glad | | |
| glide | | |
| grin | | |
| grow | | |
| grill | | |
| glow | | |
| grab | | |
| grip | | |

Fold-line

For use with OHP, for display or to make matching cards.

| | |
|---|---|
| pram | |
| pray | |
| prick | prod |
| plum | |
| plant | |
| plan | |
| press | |
| plot | play |

Copy the words:

play      pram

plan      pray

plant      press

plot      prick

plum      prod

Write the word for each picture.

| | | |
|---|---|---|
| | | |

Draw a picture for each word.

| | | |
|---|---|---|
| pram | plant | plum |

Where do you like to play?

_____

_____

_____

| YEAR Term 1 2 | SET Sheet 15 C | **LEARN, WRITE, CHECK.** ● Initial Consonant Clusters | Name: _ _ _ _ _ _ _ _ _ _ _ _ |

| Learn the word | Write then cover | Write then check |
|---|---|---|
| pram | | |
| pray | | |
| prick | | |
| prod | | |
| plum | | |
| plant | | |
| plan | | |
| press | | |
| plot | | |
| play | | |

Fold-line

● **Initial Consonant Clusters**

For use
with OHP,
for display
or
to make
matching
cards.

scar

scarf

scrap

screen

screw

scales

scrub

scooter

scab

scruffy

Copy the words:

scab _____    scrap _____

scar _____    scrub _____

scarf _____    screen _____

scales _____    screw _____

scooter _____    scruffy _____

Write the word for each picture.

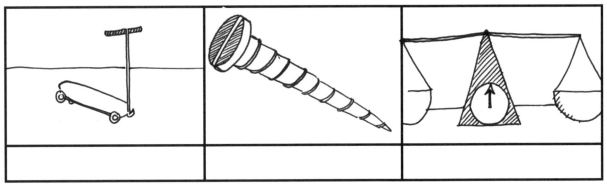

Write the missing word then copy the sentence:

The girl is wearing a hat and a _____ .

_____

_____

Draw a boy on a scooter.

Name: _____   **LEARN, WRITE, CHECK.**   YEAR Term | SET Sheet
● Initial Consonant Clusters   1   2 | 16   C

| Learn the word | Write then cover | Write then check |
|---|---|---|
| scar | | |
| scarf | | |
| scrap | | |
| screen | | |
| screw | | |
| scales | | |
| scrub | | |
| scooter | | |
| scab | | |
| scruffy | | |

Fold-line

skip

ski

skin

slab

skirt

sleep

slug

skates

skid

slip

For use
with OHP,
for display
or
to make
matching
cards.

Copy the words:

ski               skates

skid            slab

skip             sleep

skin            slip

skirt          slug

Write the word for each picture.

Draw a picture of you asleep in bed.

What time do you go to bed?  Describe your bedtime.

_____

_____

_____

_____

| YEAR Term | SET Sheet | |
|---|---|---|
| 1 2 | 17 C | |

**LEARN, WRITE, CHECK.**
● **Initial Consonant Clusters**

Name: _ _ _ _ _ _ _ _ _ _ _ _ _

| Learn the word | Write then cover | Write then check |
|---|---|---|
| skip | | |
| ski | | |
| skin | | |
| slab | | |
| skirt | | |
| sleep | | |
| slug | | |
| skates | | |
| skid | | |
| slip | | |

Fold-line

spade

smell

snap

spot

smile

snow

spider

spoon

small

sniff

Copy the words:

small          snow

smell          spot

smile          spoon

snap           spade

sniff          spider

Write the word for each picture.

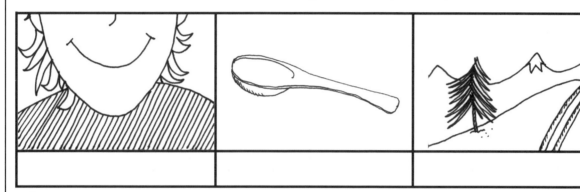

Draw a picture for each word.

| | | |
|---|---|---|
| spade | spider | spot |

Write the missing word then copy the sentence:

I eat jelly with a_____ .

_____

| Learn the word | Write then cover | Write then check |
|----------------|------------------|------------------|
| spade | | |
| smell | | |
| snap | | |
| spot | | |
| smile | | |
| snow | | |
| spider | | |
| spoon | | |
| small | | |
| sniff | | |

Fold-line

YEAR
**1**
Term
**2**

SET
**19**
Sheet
**A**

For use
with OHP,
for display
or
to make
matching
cards.

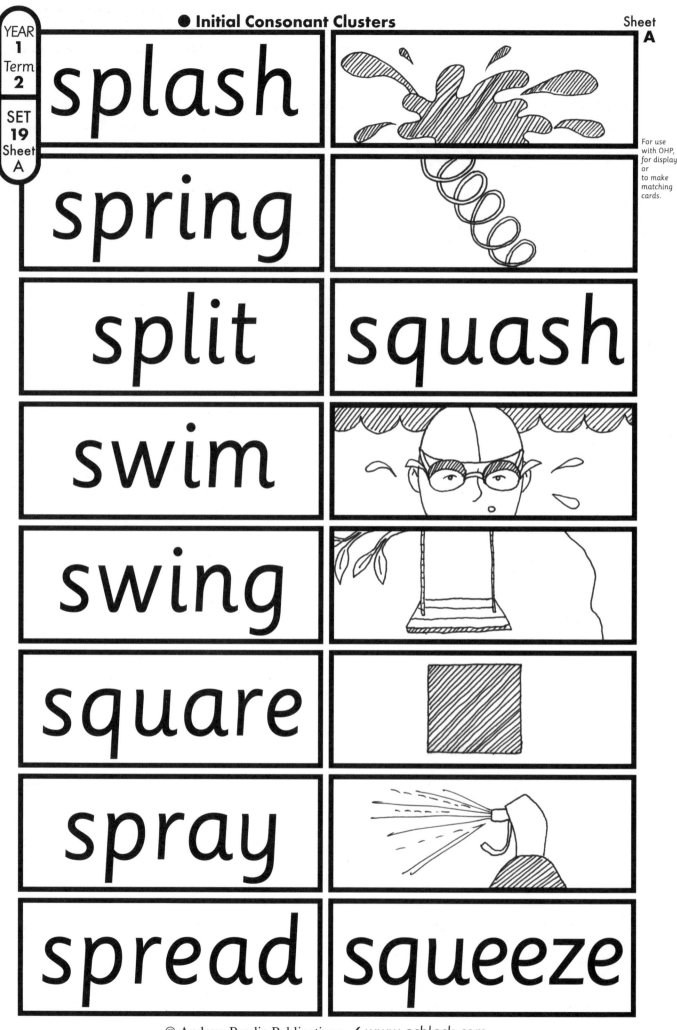

splash

spring

split

squash

swim

swing

square

spray

spread

squeeze

Copy the words:

splash _____    square _____

split _____    squash _____

spray _____    squeeze _____

spread _____    swim _____

spring _____    swing _____

Write the missing word, then copy the sentence:

We _____ butter on bread.

_____

_____

This is a _____.

_____

Draw four squares. Colour each one.

**LEARN, WRITE, CHECK.**
● **Initial Consonant Clusters**

Name: _____

| Learn the word | Write then cover | Write then check |
|---|---|---|
| splash | | |
| spring | | |
| split | | |
| squash | | |
| swim | | |
| swing | | |
| square | | |
| spray | | |
| spread | | |
| squeeze | | |

Fold-line

YEAR
1
Term
2

SET
20
Sheet
A

For use
with OHP,
for display
or
to make
matching
cards.

| tree | |
| train | |
| trot | twin |
| twig | |
| twenty | 20 |
| tractor | |
| twist | |
| trip | trap |

Name: _ _ _ _ _ _ _ _ _ _ _

**Spelling Activity Sheet** Sheet
B

Copy the words:

train                    trot

tractor                  twins

trap                     twig

trip                     twenty

tree                     twist

Write the word for each picture.

Draw a picture for
each word.

tree

tractor

train

| Learn the word | Write then cover | Write then check |
|---|---|---|
| tree | | |
| train | | |
| trot | | |
| twin | | |
| twig | | |
| twenty | | |
| tractor | | |
| twist | | |
| trip | | |
| trap | | |

Fold-line

For use
with OHP,
for display
or
to make
matching
cards.

three

3

throat

this

they

throw

shoe

shirt

ship

shop

these

Copy the words:

| | |
|---|---|
| this | she |
| they | shop |
| three | shoe |
| throw | ship |
| throat | shirt |

Draw a ship.

Write about the ship.

_____

_____

_____

_____

_____

**LEARN, WRITE, CHECK.**
● Initial Consonant Clusters

Name: _ _ _ _ _ _ _ _ _ _ _ _

| Learn the word | Write then cover | Write then check |
|---|---|---|
| three | | |
| throat | | |
| this | | |
| they | | |
| throw | | |
| shoe | | |
| shirt | | |
| ship | | |
| shop | | |
| these | | |

Fold-line

For use
with OHP,
for display
or
to make
matching
cards.

YEAR
**1**
Term
**2**

SET
**22**
Sheet
**A**

there

where

Here ?    There ?

them

that

what

?

chair

chin

church

when

then

Copy the words:

that             when

then            where

them          church

there         chin

what          chair

Write the missing words, then copy the sentence:

In front of the _____
there is a _____.

_____

_____

The boy has a spot on his _____.

_____

_____

Draw a cat on a chair.

Name: _____          **LEARN, WRITE, CHECK.**
● **Initial Consonant Clusters**

| Learn the word | Write then cover | Write then check |
|---|---|---|
| there | | |
| where | | |
| them | | |
| that | | |
| what | | |
| chair | | |
| chin | | |
| church | | |
| when | | |
| then | | |

Fold-line

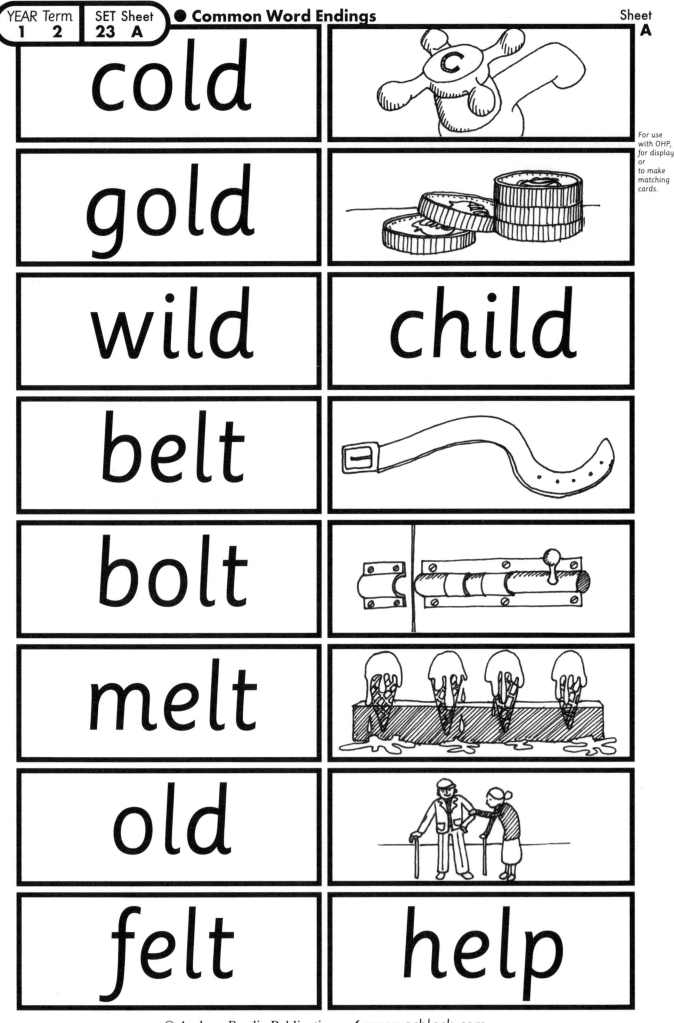

cold

gold

wild

child

belt

bolt

melt

old

felt

help

Copy the words:

old                belt

cold               bolt

gold               felt

child              melt

wild               help

Hot                          Cold

What is the weather like today?

_____

_____

Draw a picture of someone
who helps you.

Write about the person.

_____

_____

_____

**LEARN, WRITE, CHECK.**
● **Common Word Endings**

Name: _ _ _ _ _ _ _ _ _ _ _ _

| Learn the word | Write then cover | Write then check |
|:---:|:---:|:---:|
| cold | | |
| gold | | |
| wild | | |
| child | | |
| belt | | |
| bolt | | |
| melt | | |
| old | | |
| felt | | |
| help | | |

Fold-line

● **Common Word Endings**

For use
with OHP,
for display
or
to make
matching
cards.

| | |
|---|---|
| hand | |
| sand | |
| kind | find |
| pond | |
| milk | |
| calf | |
| half | |
| and | next |

Copy the words:

and                    pond

hand                   next

sand                   milk

find                   calf

kind                   half

Write the missing word, then copy the sentence:

The castle is made of

_____ .

_____

_____

Draw your hand.

Write about your picture.

_____

_____

_____

| Learn the word | Write then cover | Write then check |
| --- | --- | --- |
| hand | | |
| sand | | |
| kind | | |
| find | | |
| pond | | |
| milk | | |
| calf | | |
| half | | |
| and | | |
| next | | |

Fold-line

camp

lamp

jump

thank

stamp

pink

drink

act

fact

think

For use with OHP, for display or to make matching cards.

Copy the words:

camp _____     fact _____
lamp _____     pink _____
stamp _____     think _____
jump _____     drink _____
act _____     thank _____

Write about the pictures.

**LEARN, WRITE, CHECK.**
● **Common Word Endings**

Name: _ _ _ _ _ _ _ _ _ _ _ _

| Learn the word | Write then cover | Write then check |
|---|---|---|
| camp | | |
| lamp | | |
| jump | | |
| thank | | |
| stamp | | |
| pink | | |
| drink | | |
| act | | |
| fact | | |
| think | | |

*Fold-line*

Sheet
**A**

● **Common Word Endings**

YEAR
**1**
Term
**2**

SET
**26**
Sheet
**A**

For use
with OHP,
for display
or
to make
matching
cards.

| | |
|---|---|
| *left* | |
| *lift* | |
| *lunch* | *bunch* |
| *mask* | |
| *branch* | |
| *bench* | |
| *filth* | |
| *ask* | *crunch* |

Name: _____

Copy the words:

left _____

lift _____

lunch _____

bunch _____

crunch _____

branch _____

bench _____

ask _____

mask _____

filth _____

Write about the pictures.

_____
_____
_____
_____

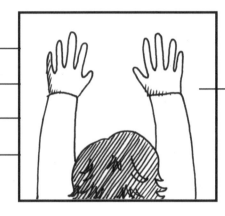

This is
her right
hand.

This is a _____
of bananas.
_____

The boy is sitting on a
_____ . He is
eating his _____ .

| Learn the word | Write then cover | Write then check |
|---|---|---|
| left | | |
| lift | | |
| lunch | | |
| bunch | | |
| mask | | |
| branch | | |
| bench | | |
| filth | | |
| ask | | |
| crunch | | |

*Fold-line*

vest

For use
with OHP,
for display
or
to make
matching
cards.

dust

just

kept

must

post

list

last

best

most

fast

Copy the words:

kept _____     must _____

last _____     most _____

fast _____     just _____

best _____     list _____

vest _____     post _____

Write the missing word, then copy the sentence:

The girl will _____ the letter.

_____

_____

The car is going _____ .

_____

My dog is good.

My dog is the _____ .

**LEARN, WRITE, CHECK.**
● Common Word Endings

Name: _ _ _ _ _ _ _ _ _ _ _ _ _

| Learn the word | Write then cover | Write then check |
|---|---|---|
| vest | | |
| fast | | |
| kept | | |
| must | | |
| post | | |
| list | | |
| last | | |
| best | | |
| most | | |
| just | | |

Fold-line

Sheet
A

● **Long Vowel Phonemes**

YEAR
**1** & **2**
Term
**3** **1**

SET
**28**
Sheet
**A**

For use with OHP, for display or to make matching cards.

sweet

tea

been

asleep

sea

leaf

seat

read

seen

street

Name: _ _ _ _ _ _ _ _ _ _

**Spelling Activity Sheet** Sheet

B

Copy the words:

been _____     tea _____

seen _____     sea _____

sweet _____    seat _____

street _____   leaf _____

asleep _____   read _____

Write about your pictures.

Draw a sweet.

_____

_____

Draw a leaf.

_____

_____

_____

Draw yourself asleep.

_____

_____

_____

Name: _____

**LEARN, WRITE, CHECK.**
● **Long Vowel Phonemes**

YEAR Term
& 1   3
  2   1

SET Sheet
28   C

| Learn the word | Write then cover | Write then check |
|---|---|---|
| sweet | | |
| tea | | |
| been | | |
| asleep | | |
| sea | | |
| leaf | | |
| seat | | |
| read | | |
| seen | | |
| street | | |

Fold-line

For use with OHP, for display or to make matching cards.

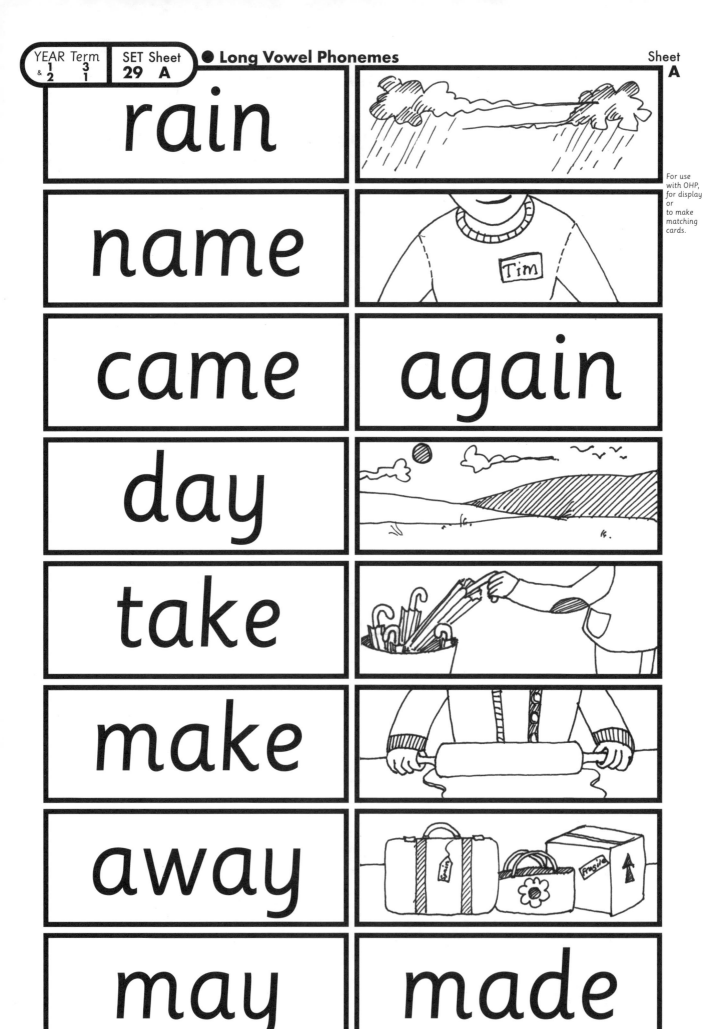

rain

name

came | again

day

take

make

away

may | made

Copy the words:

rain _____     make _____

again _____    take _____

name _____     day _____

came _____     may _____

made _____     away _____

Write the missing words to answer the question, then copy the sentence:

What is your name?

My _____ is _____.

_____

Write the missing word, then copy the sentence:

The —————— is falling.

_____

_____

Fill in the missing words in this rhyme.

Rain, _____ , go _____ ,
Come_____ another day.
Rain,_____ , go_____ ,
Come on mother's washing _____.

Week 2 Year 2.

**LEARN, WRITE, CHECK.**
● **Long Vowel Phonemes**

Name: _____

| Learn the word | Write then cover | Write then check |
|---|---|---|
| rain | | |
| name | | |
| came | | |
| again | | |
| day | | |
| take | | |
| make | | |
| away | | |
| may | | |
| made | | |

*Fold-line*

● **Long Vowel Phonemes**

YEAR
**1** & **2**
Term
**3  1**

SET
**30**
Sheet
**A**

For use
with OHP,
for display
or
to make
matching
cards.

pie

tie

nice

time

mice

night

bike

fly

try

by

Copy the words:

pie _____    bike _____

tie _____    time _____

fly _____    mice _____

try _____    nice _____

by _____    night _____

Write the missing word,
then copy the sentence:

This is a _____ .

_____

Draw a picture of you on a bike.
Write about your picture.

_____

_____

_____

_____

Week 3 Year 2

Name: _____    **LEARN, WRITE, CHECK.**    | YEAR Term | SET Sheet |
● **Long Vowel Phonemes**    | & 1 2   3 1 | 30   C |

| Learn the word | Write then cover | Write then check |
|---|---|---|
| pie | | |
| tie | | |
| nice | | |
| time | | |
| mice | | |
| night | | |
| bike | | |
| fly | | |
| try | | |
| by | | |

Fold-line

YEAR Term
& 1 3
2 1

SET Sheet
31 A

● Long Vowel Phonemes

Sheet
A

For use
with OHP,
for display
or
to make
matching
cards.

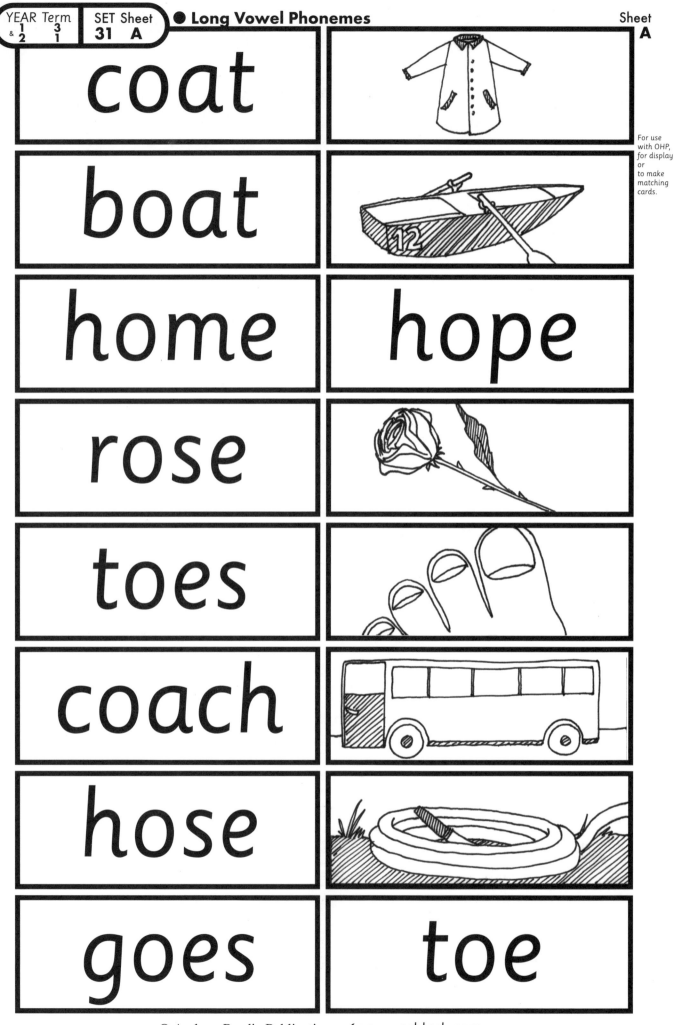

coat

boat

home

hope

rose

toes

coach

hose

goes

toe

Copy the words:

coat             hose

boat             rose

coach          toe

home           toes

hope            goes

Draw your home.

Write about your home.

Write about this picture.

| YEAR Term & 1 3 2 1 | SET Sheet 31 C | LEARN, WRITE, CHECK. ● Long Vowel Phonemes | Name: _ _ _ _ _ _ _ _ _ _ _ _ |

| Learn the word | Write then cover | Write then check |
|---|---|---|
| coat | | |
| boat | | |
| home | | |
| hope | | |
| rose | | |
| toes | | |
| coach | | |
| hose | | |
| goes | | |
| toe | | |

*Fold-line*

● **Long Vowel Phonemes**

YEAR
**1** & **2**
Term
**3** **1**

SET
**32**
Sheet
**A**

# boot

# school

# too

# soon

# tooth

# blue

# room

# new

# grew

# June

Copy the words:

boot                  school

room              blue

soon                new

tooth            grew

too                 June

Write the missing word, then copy the sentence:

My new_____grew in June.

_____.

Draw your bedroom.

Write about your room.

_____

_____

_____

_____

Name: _____

**LEARN, WRITE, CHECK.**
● Long Vowel Phonemes

| YEAR Term | | SET Sheet |
|---|---|---|
| 1 & 2 | 3 1 | 32  C |

| Learn the word | Write then cover | Write then check |
|---|---|---|
| 6  school | | |
| 8  too | | |
| 2  soon | | |
| 4  tooth | | |
| 3  blue | | |
| 7  room | | |
| 9  new | | |
| 5  grew | | |
| 10  June | | |
| 1  boot | | |

*Fold-line*

For use with OHP, for display or to make matching cards.

| | |
|---|---|
| an | as |
| can | can't |
| do | don't |
| is | isn't |
| be | because |
| him | night |
| or | so |
| want | said |

Copy the words:

is _____    want _____
isn't _____    can't _____
because _____    do _____
night _____    don't _____
him _____    said _____

Write the missing word, then copy the sentence:

This door ___ open.

_____

This door ___ open.

_____

Write about the picture.

_____
_____
_____
_____

Week 6 - Yr 2

**LEARN, WRITE, CHECK.**
● Useful Extra Words

Name: _ _ _ _ _ _ _ _ _ _ _ _

| Learn the word | Write then cover | Write then check |
|---|---|---|
| 1. an | | |
| 2. as | | |
| 4 can | | |
| 9. can't | | |
| 12 do | | |
| 6 don't | | |
| 8. is | | |
| 11 isn't | | |
| 13 be | | |
| 2. because | | |
| 4 him | | |
| 5 night | | |
| 13. or | | |
| 16 so | | |
| 7. want | | |
| 10 said | | |

Fold-line

● **Useful Extra Words**

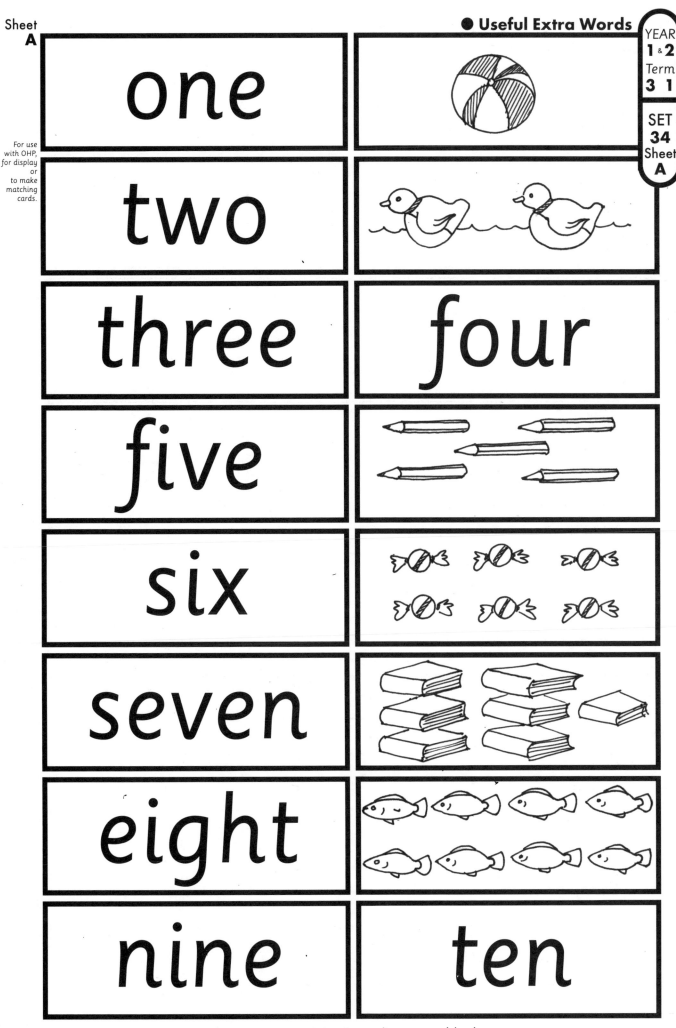

one

two

three

four

five

six

seven

eight

nine

ten

Copy the words:

| | |
|---|---|
| one _____ | six _____ |
| two _____ | seven _____ |
| three _____ | eight _____ |
| four _____ | nine _____ |
| five _____ | ten _____ |

Write the word for each picture.

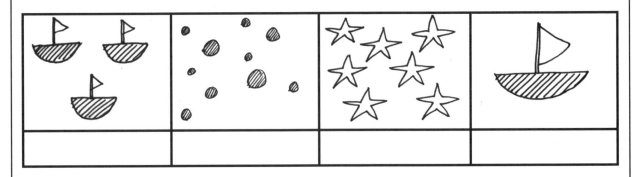

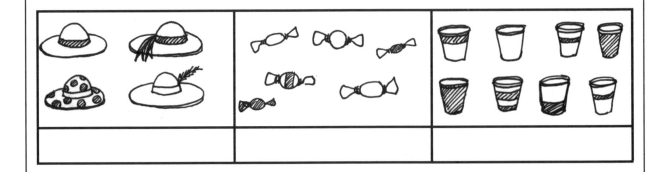

Name:_____

| Learn the word | Write then cover | Write then check |
|---|---|---|
| one | | |
| two | | |
| three | | |
| four | | |
| five | | |
| six | | |
| seven | | |
| eight | | |
| nine | | |
| ten | | |

Fold-line

● **Vowel Phonemes**

YEAR
2
Term
1

SET
35
Sheet
A

Sheet
**A**

For use
with OHP,
for display
or
to make
matching
cards.

look

book

cook

took

foot

wood

hood

cooking

stood

looking

Copy the words:

look          cooking

book          foot

cook          hood

took          stood

looking       wood

Write about the picture.

_____
_____
_____
_____
_____
_____
_____

**LEARN, WRITE, CHECK.**
● **Vowel Phonemes**

Name: _ _ _ _ _ _ _ _ _ _ _ _ _

| Learn the word | Write then cover | Write then check |
|---|---|---|
| look | | |
| book | | |
| cook | | |
| took | | |
| foot | | |
| wood | | |
| hood | | |
| cooking | | |
| stood | | |
| looking | | |

Fold-line

● Vowel Phonemes

YEAR 2 Term 1

SET 36 Sheet A

For use with OHP, for display or to make matching cards.

car

card

carpet

farmer

star

farm

shark

garden

sharp

market

Name: _ _ _ _ _ _ _ _ _ _ _

**Spelling Activity Sheet**  Sheet

**B**

Copy the words:

car _____        farm _____

card _____        farmer _____

carpet _____        sharp _____

garden _____        shark _____

market _____        star _____

There is something strange in this picture.

Write about the picture.

_____

_____

_____

_____

_____

_____

_____

Name: _____    **LEARN, WRITE, CHECK.**
● **Vowel Phonemes**

| YEAR Term | SET Sheet |
|---|---|
| 2  1 | 36  C |

| Learn the word | Write then cover | Write then check |
|---|---|---|
| car | | |
| card | | |
| carpet | | |
| farmer | | |
| star | | |
| farm | | |
| shark | | |
| garden | | |
| sharp | | |
| market | | |

Fold-line

boy

toy

enjoy

annoy

royal

oil

coin

noisy

voice

noise

For use
with OHP,
for display
or
to make
matching
cards.

Copy the words:

boy _____     oil _____

toy _____     coin _____

enjoy _____     noise _____

annoy _____     noisy _____

royal _____     voice _____

vrooom!

Write about the picture.

_____

_____

_____

_____

_____

_____

_____

20.11.06

**LEARN, WRITE, CHECK.**
● **Vowel Phonemes**

Name: _____

| Learn the word | Write then cover | Write then check |
|---|---|---|
| boy ^1 | | |
| toy ^9. | | |
| enjoy ^2 | | |
| annoy ^8. | | |
| royal ^3 | | |
| oil ^4. | | |
| coin ^5. | | |
| noisy ^6. | | |
| voice ^7. | | |
| noise ^10, | | |

Fold-line

© Andrew Brodie Publications ✓ www.acblack.com

● **Vowel Phonemes**

For use
with OHP,
for display
or
to make
matching
cards.

# owl

# town

# how

# down

# frown

# crown

# shower

# flower

# now

# crowd

Copy the words:

| | |
|---|---|
| how | frown |
| now | crown |
| owl | crowd |
| down | shower |
| town | flower |

Find something strange in the picture.

Write about the picture.

_____
_____
_____
_____
_____
_____
_____
_____

24.11.06

Name: _____   **LEARN, WRITE, CHECK.**
● **Vowel Phonemes**

| YEAR | Term | SET | Sheet |
|------|------|-----|-------|
| 2 | 1 | 38 | C |

| Learn the word | | Write then cover | Write then check |
|---|---|---|---|
| owl | 3. | | |
| town | 5. *Fold-line* | | |
| how | 6. | | |
| down | 2. | | |
| frown | 4 | | |
| crown | 8 | | |
| shower | 1. | | |
| flower | 7. | | |
| now | 10. | | |
| crowd | 9 | | |

For use
with OHP,
for display
or
to make
matching
cards.

mouse

house

out

about

shout

pound

mouth

count

loud

thousand

Copy the words:

out _____     loud _____

about _____     mouth _____

shout _____     pound _____

house _____     count _____

mouse _____     thousand _____

Fill in the missing words.

A _____ is a very big number.

I have teeth in my _____ .

My _____ has got three bedrooms.

I went _____ for a walk.

Don't _____ out _____ .

1.12.06

**LEARN, WRITE, CHECK.**
● **Vowel Phonemes**

Name:_____

| Learn the word | Write then cover | Write then check |
|---|---|---|
| mouse | | |
| house | | |
| out | | |
| about | | |
| shout | | |
| pound | | |
| mouth | | |
| count | | |
| loud | | |
| thousand | | |

Fold-line

# Monday

# Tuesday

# Wednesday

# Thursday

# Friday

# Saturday

# Sunday

# today

Name: _ _ _ _ _ _ _ _ _

Copy the words:

Monday _____    Saturday _____

Tuesday _____    Sunday _____

Wednesday _____    today _____

Thursday _____    yesterday _____

Friday _____    holiday _____

Fill in the missing words.

Today is _____ .

Yesterday was _____ .

Write about yesterday.
What day was it?  What happened yesterday?

_____

_____

_____

_____

_____

_____

_____

_____

_____

3. 12. 06

Name: _____

**LEARN, WRITE, CH**
● **Days of the W**

SET Sheet
41

YEAR Term
2    1

| Learn the word | Write then cover | |
|---|---|---|
| Monday | | |
| Tuesday | | |
| Wednesday | | |
| Thursday | | |
| Friday | | |
| Saturday | | |
| Sunday | | |
| today | | |
| yesterday | | |
| holiday | | |

Fold-line

For use
with OHP,
for display
or
to make
matching
cards.

you

they

get          after

going

push

over

went

getting          are

Copy the words:

you                      get

they                  getting

are                     went

after                push

going               over

Find something strange in the picture.

Write about the picture.

_____

_____

_____

_____

_____

_____

**LEARN, WRITE, CHECK.**
● **Useful Extra Words**

Name: _ _ _ _ _ _ _ _ _ _ _

| Learn the word | Write then cover | Write then check |
|---|---|---|
| 6. you | | |
| 4. they | | |
| 5. get | | |
| 9. after | | |
| 7 going | | |
| 3 push | | |
| 2 over | | |
| 1 went | | |
| 8. getting | | |
| 10 are | | |

Fold-line

Sheet
A

● **Vowel Phonemes**

YEAR
**2**
Term
**2**

SET
**42**
Sheet
**A**

For use
with OHP,
for display
or
to make
matching
cards.

| | |
|---|---|
| fair | |
| hair | |
| pair | air |
| repair | |
| chair | |
| stairs | |
| fairy | |
| there | where |

Copy the words:

air                          chair

fair                         stairs

hair                         fairy

pair                         there

repair                       where

Look carefully at the picture.

Write about the picture.

_____

_____

_____

_____

_____

_____

Name: _____ **LEARN, WRITE, CHECK.** ● Vowel Phonemes

| | YEAR Term | SET Sheet |
|---|---|---|
| | 2   2 | 42   C |

| Learn the word | Write then cover | Write then check |
|---|---|---|
| fair | | |
| hair | | |
| pair | | |
| air | | |
| repair | | |
| chair | | |
| stairs | | |
| fairy | | |
| there | | |
| where | | |

Fold-line

© Andrew Brodie Publications ✓ www.acblack.com

For use
with OHP,
for display
or
to make
matching
cards.

pear

bear

wear

their

tear

stare

scare

care

share

square

Copy the words:

care _____     pear _____

scare _____    bear _____

stare _____    tear _____

share _____    wear _____

square _____    their _____

Fill in the missing words:

I cannot _____ my shirt because it has a _____ in it.

Some people don't_____ _____ sweets with others.

Draw a red square, a blue square and a yellow square.

a red _____          a yellow _____

a blue _____

8.1.07

# LEARN, WRITE, CHECK.
● Vowel Phonemes

Name: _ _ _ _ _ _ _ _ _ _ _ _

| Learn the word | Write then cover | Write then check |
|---|---|---|
| pear _2_ | | |
| bear _6_ | | |
| wear _4_ | | |
| their _8_ | | |
| tear _9_ | | |
| stare _1_ | | |
| scare _5._ | | |
| care _10_ | | |
| share _7_ | | |
| square _3_ | | |

Fold-line

© Andrew Brodie Publications ✓ www.acblack.com

Sheet
A

● Vowel Phonemes

YEAR
2
Term
2

SET
44
Sheet
A

For use
with OHP,
for display
or
to make
matching
cards.

fork

horse

born

sport

morning

forty

door

story

floor

poor

Name: _ _ _ _ _ _ _ _ _ _ _

Copy the words:

fork _____     horse _____

born _____     sport _____

morning _____    poor _____

forty _____    door _____

story _____    floor _____

Answer the questions.

When were you born?

_____

What is your favourite sport?

_____

What have you done this morning?

_____

Write about your favourite story.

_____

_____

_____

_____

_____

_____

| Learn the word | Write then cover | Write then check |
|----------------|------------------|------------------|
| fork | | |
| horse | | |
| born | | |
| sport | | |
| morning | | |
| forty | | |
| door | | |
| story | | |
| floor | | |
| poor | | |

Fold-line

saw

claw

yawn

dawn

autumn

sauce

paw

caught

taught

crawl

For use
with OHP,
for display
or
to make
matching
cards.

Copy the words:

saw _____    crawl _____

paw _____    sauce _____

claw _____    autumn _____

dawn _____    caught _____

yawn _____    taught _____

Describe the cat. What are her ears like? What are her paws like?

_____
_____
_____
_____
_____
_____

Draw a dog, then describe it.

_____
_____
_____
_____
_____
_____
_____
_____

**LEARN, WRITE, CHECK.**
● Vowel Phonemes

Name: _____

| Learn the word | Write then cover | Write then check |
|---|---|---|
| saw | | |
| claw | | |
| yawn | | |
| dawn | | |
| autumn | | |
| sauce | | |
| paw | | |
| caught | | |
| taught | | |
| crawl | | |

Fold-line

● **Vowel Phonemes**

| | |
|---|---|
| core | |
| snore | |
| more | store |
| explore | |
| sore | |
| tore | |
| bored | |
| before | wore |

Copy the words:

more _____          snore _____

core _____          store _____

sore _____          before _____

tore _____          explore _____

wore _____          bored _____

Answer these Questions:

What did you wear yesterday?

_____

_____

Question: What number comes just before six?

Answer:

The number just before six is _____.

Question: What number comes just before ten?

Answer:

_____ comes just before ten.

Question: What day comes just before Monday?

Answer:

_____ comes before Monday.

Question: What month comes just before June?

Answer:

_____ comes just before June.

| Learn the word | Write then cover | Write then check |
|---|---|---|
| 8. core | | |
| 5. snore | | |
| 2. more | | |
| 3. store | | |
| 1. explore | | |
| 4. sore | | |
| 6. tore | | |
| 7. bored | | |
| 9. before | | |
| 10 wore | | |

Fold-line

# bigger

## brother

## her

## were

## over

## under

## sister

## water

## other

## another

For use
with OHP,
for display
or
to make
matching
cards.

Copy the words:

| | |
|---|---|
| her | brother |
| over | sister |
| under | were |
| other | bigger |
| another | water |

Draw the people in your family.

Describe the people in your family.

_____

_____

_____

_____

_____

_____

_____

| Learn the word | Write then cover | Write then check |
|---|---|---|
| bigger 2. | | |
| brother 1. | | |
| her 9. | | |
| were 3. | | |
| over 4 | | |
| under 5 | | |
| sister 6. | | |
| water 7. | | |
| other 8. | | |
| another 10. | | |

*Fold-line*

● **Vowel Phonemes**

For use
with OHP,
for display
or
to make
matching
cards.

| | |
|---|---|
| bird | |
| girl | |
| first | third |
| circle | |
| stir | |
| dirty | |
| thirty | 30 |
| thirsty | thirteen |

Copy the words:

| | |
|---|---|
| bird | third |
| girl | first |
| stir | thirty |
| dirty | thirteen |
| thirsty | circle |

Draw a picture for each word.

| | | | |
|---|---|---|---|
| | | | |
| bird | girl | dirty | stir |

The boy with the triangle on his shirt came second in the race.
Write about the other two people.

_____

_____

Name: _____    **LEARN, WRITE, CHECK.**
● **Vowel Phonemes**

| Learn the word | Write then cover | Write then check |
|---|---|---|
| bird | | |
| girl | | |
| first | | |
| third | | |
| circle | | |
| stir | | |
| dirty | | |
| thirty | | |
| thirsty | | |
| thirteen | | |

Fold-line

fur

curl

curve | purpose

nurse

burn

curtains

hurt

return | surprise

For use
with OHP,
for display
or
to make
matching
cards.

Copy the words:

fur _____      nurse _____

curl _____      return _____

burn _____      purpose _____

hurt _____      surprise _____

curve _____      curtains _____

Fill in the missing words.

We open the _____ in the morning.

If you _____ yourself on the cooker it will _____ a lot. You might have to go to hospital to see a _____ or a doctor.

My birthday present was a big _____.
The new plate was broken so we had to _____ it to the shop.

My sister was naughty because she dropped her glass on _____.

Draw a cat with black fur.

**LEARN, WRITE, CHECK.**
● **Vowel Phonemes**

Name: _ _ _ _ _ _ _ _ _ _ _ _

| Learn the word | Write then cover | Write then check |
|---|---|---|
| fur  *7* | | |
| curl  *4*  Fold-line | | |
| curve  *8* | | |
| purpose  *1.* | | |
| nurse  *2* | | |
| burn  *10* | | |
| curtains  *3* | | |
| hurt  *6* | | |
| return  *5.* | | |
| surprise  *9* | | |

Sheet
A

● **Vowel Phonemes**

YEAR
2
Term
3

SET
50
Sheet
A

For use
with OHP,
for display
or
to make
matching
cards.

| | |
|---|---|
| ear | |
| hear | |
| near | clear |
| tear | |
| beard | |
| fear | |
| disappear | |
| appear | dear |

Copy the words:

ear _____    fear _____

hear _____    beard _____

near _____    clear _____

tear _____    appear _____

dear _____    disappear _____

Choose the correct words to label the picture.

hair
eye
nose
beard
ear
mouth

_____

_____

_____

_____

_____

_____

Draw your own face
and label the picture.
Remember that you
haven't got a beard!

| Learn the word | Write then cover | Write then check |
|----------------|------------------|------------------|
| ear | | |
| hear | | |
| near | | |
| clear | | |
| tear | | |
| beard | | |
| fear | | |
| disappear | | |
| appear | | |
| dear | | |

YEAR
**2**
Term
**3**

SET
**51**
Sheet
**A**

head

bread

instead · tread

spread

feather

heavy

weather

ready · steady

© Andrew Brodie Publications ✓ www.acblack.com

Copy the words:

head                    ready
bread                   steady
spread                  weather
tread                   feather
instead                 heavy

Fill in the missing words then answer the questions.

Do you like to _____ butter on your _____?

_____

What is the _____ like today?
(Is it sunny or rainy?)

_____

Do you sometimes wear a hat on your _____?

_____

Is your bag very _____, or is it light?

_____

**LEARN, WRITE, CHECK.**
● Vowel Phonemes

Name: _____

| Learn the word | Write then cover | Write then check |
|---|---|---|
| head 5. | | |
| bread 1 | | |
| instead 6. | | |
| tread 7 | | |
| spread 2 | | |
| feather 3 | | |
| heavy 4. | | |
| weather 10 | | |
| ready 9 | | |
| steady 8 | | |

Fold-line

Sheet
A

● **Numbers 11-20**

YEAR
**2**
Term
**3**

SET
**52**
Sheet
**A**

For use
with OHP,
for display
or
to make
matching
cards.

eleven 11

twelve 12

thirteen 13

fourteen 14

fifteen 15

sixteen 16

seventeen 17

eighteen 18

nineteen 19

twenty 20

Name: _ _ _ _ _ _ _ _ _ _ _ _

Copy the words:

eleven                          sixteen

twelve                          seventeen

thirteen                        eighteen

fourteen                        nineteen

fifteen                         twenty

Write the correct words under the pictures.

Name: _____ **LEARN, WRITE, CHECK.**
● **Numbers 11-20**

| Learn the word | Write then cover | Write then check |
|---|---|---|
| *2* eleven | | |
| *6* twelve | | |
| *1* thirteen | | |
| *3* fourteen | | |
| *4* fifteen | | |
| *5* sixteen | | |
| *8* seventeen | | |
| *7* eighteen | | |
| nineteen | | |
| *9* twenty | | |

*Fold-line*

For use
with OHP,
for display
or
to make
matching
cards.

red

orange

yellow | green

blue

purple

pink

brown

black | white

Copy the words:

red                                    purple

orange                            pink

yellow                            brown

green                              black

blue                                white

Using one colour at a time, draw a picture in each large box.
Write the colour under the box.

**LEARN, WRITE, CHECK.**
● **Colours**

Name: _ _ _ _ _ _ _ _ _ _ _ _

| Learn the word | Write then cover | Write then check |
|----------------|------------------|------------------|
| red        4   |                  |                  |
| orange     5   |                  |                  |
| yellow     3   |                  |                  |
| green      2   |                  |                  |
| blue       6   |                  |                  |
| purple     1   |                  |                  |
| pink       7   |                  |                  |
| brown      9   |                  |                  |
| black      10  |                  |                  |
| white      8   |                  |                  |

Fold-line

# laugh

# little

# some

# went

# come

# called

# with

# could

# should

# have

# would

# here

Name: _ _ _ _ _ _ _ _ _ _ _

**Spelling Activity Sheet** Sheet

**B**

Copy the words:

some _____        could _____

come _____        should _____

went _____        would _____

with _____        have _____

called _____       laugh _____

here _____        little _____

Write about a day out with a friend. Use some of the words from the list above.

_____

_____

_____

_____

_____

_____

_____

_____

_____

_____

_____

_____

_____

_____

Name: _____

**LEARN, WRITE, CHECK.**
● **Extra Useful Words**

YEAR Term
2    3

SET Sheet
54   C

| Learn the word | Write then cover | Write then check |
|---|---|---|
| 2. laugh | | |
| 6. little | | |
| 1. some | | |
| 7. went | | |
| 9. come | | |
| 3. called | | |
| 4 with | | |
| 5 could | | |
| 8 should | | |
| 10. have | | |
| 12 would | | |
| 11 here | | |

Fold-line

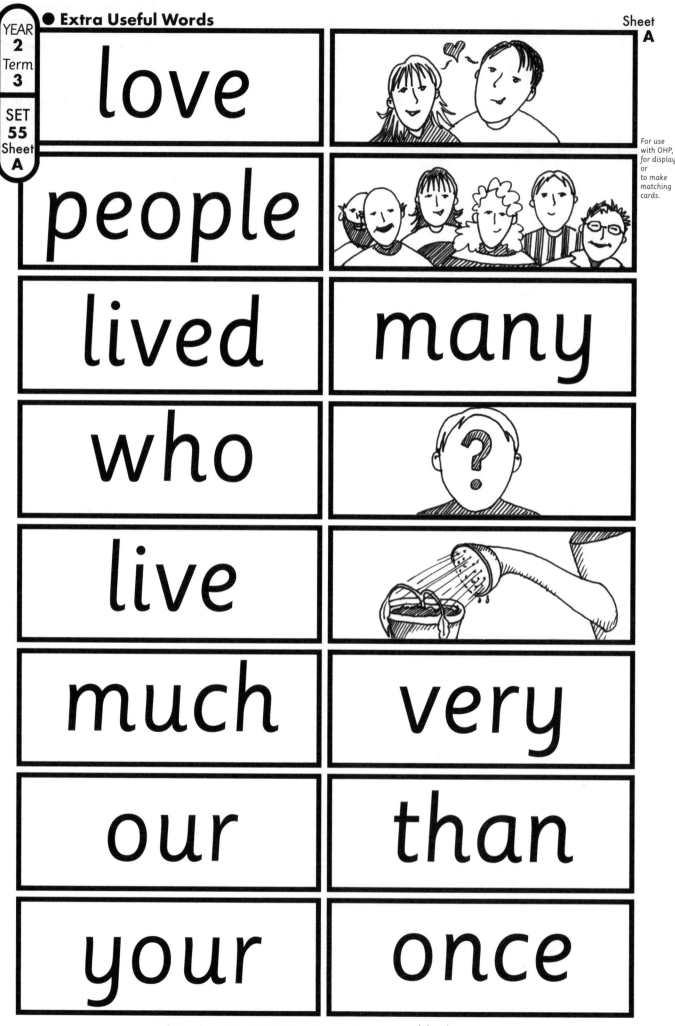

For use with OHP, for display or to make matching cards.

love

people

lived        many

who          ?

live

much         very

our          than

your         once

Copy the words:

live _____    our _____

lived _____    people _____

love _____    than _____

many _____    very _____

much _____    who _____

once _____    your _____

Fill in the missing words, then answer the questions.

Some _____ live by the sea and some people live a long way from the sea. Is _____ house near the sea?

_____

_____

_____ do you sit next to in class?

_____

How _____ children are in your class?

_____

Write a sentence using this word: lived.

_____

_____

**LEARN, WRITE, CHECK.**
● **Extra Useful Words**

Name: _ _ _ _ _ _ _ _ _ _ _ _ _

| Learn the word | Write then cover | Write then check |
|----------------|------------------|------------------|
| love _2_ | | |
| people _1_ | | |
| lived _3_ | | |
| many _7_ | | |
| who _4_ | | |
| live _5_ | | |
| much _11_ | | |
| very _6_ | | |
| our _8_ | | |
| than _9_ | | |
| your _10_ | | |
| once _12_ | | |

Fold-line

YEAR
2
Term
3
SET
56
Sheet
A

# January

# February

# March

# April

# May

# June

# July

# August

# September

# October

# November

# December

Name: _ _ _ _ _ _ _ _

Copy the words:

| | |
|---|---|
| January | July |
| February | August |
| March | September |
| April | October |
| May | November |
| June | December |

Fill in the missing words.
You will need to turn the paper around to write the words.

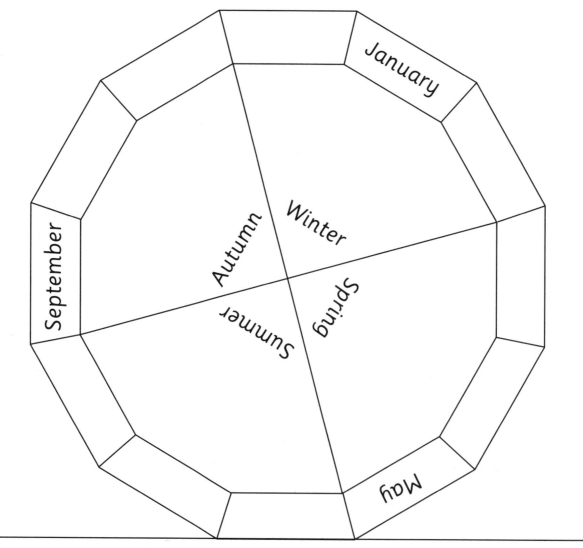

Name: _ _ _ _ _ _ _ _ _ _ _   **LEARN, WRITE, CHECK.**
● **Months of the Year**

| YEAR Term | SET Sheet |
|---|---|
| 2    3 | 56  C |

| Learn the word | Write then cover | Write then check |
|---|---|---|
| January | | |
| February | | |
| March | | |
| April | | |
| May | | |
| June | | |
| July | | |
| August | | |
| September | | |
| October | | |
| November | | |
| December | | |

# Pupil record sheet for SPELLING
(Line through word when practised. Cross when learnt.)

Pupil's name: _____

| | |
|---|---|
| Set 1 | man, van, can, ran, bat, cat, mat, hat, dad, bad |
| Set 2 | sad, bag, had, has, gas, wax, wag, tap, gap, lap |
| Set 3 | web, bed, get, ten, net, leg, red, men, wet, yes |
| Set 4 | pig, dig, did, if, bin, sit, six, his, him, it |
| Set 5 | hot, top, got, pot, hop, fox, dog, dot, not, job |
| Set 6 | cup, bug, mum, put, hug, mud, run, cut, but, us |
| Set 7 | sack, lock, neck, pick, sock, duck, back, lick, luck, peck |
| Set 8 | muff, kiss, huff, toss, mess, puff, off, miss, less, fuss |
| Set 9 | ball, tall, all, tell, hill, pull, hall, bell, will, call |
| Set 10 | sing, king, song, hung, ring, wing, long, bang, rung, hang |
| Set 11 | black, blush, blot, blast, blow, brick, brush, brown, brother, bring |
| Set 12 | crab, crack, crust, dry, crib, drip, drum, dress, drop, cross |
| Set 13 | flag, frog, flip, flop, frill, fry, frost, flat, from, fling |
| Set 14 | glass, glue, glad, glide, grin, grow, grill, glow, grab, grip |
| Set 15 | pram, pray, prick, prod, plum, plant, plan, press, plot, play |
| Set 16 | scar, scarf, scrap, screen, screw, scales, scrub, scooter, scab, scruffy |
| Set 17 | skip, ski, skin, slab, skirt, sleep, slug, skates, skid, slip |
| Set 18 | spade, smell, snap, spot, smile, snow, spider, spoon, small, sniff |
| Set 19 | splash, spring, split, squash, swim, swing, square, spray, spread, squeeze |
| Set 20 | tree, train, trot, twin, twig, twenty, tractor, twist, trip, trap |
| Set 21 | three, throat, this, they, throw, shoe, shirt, ship, shop, she |
| Set 22 | there, where, them, that, what, chair, chin, church, when, there |
| Set 23 | cold, gold, wild, child, belt, bolt, melt, old, felt, help |
| Set 24 | hand, sand, kind, find, pond, milk, calf, half, and, next |
| Set 25 | camp, lamp, jump, thank, stamp, pink, drink, act, fact, think |
| Set 26 | left, lift, lunch, bunch, mask, branch, bench, filth, ask, crunch |

| | |
|---|---|
| **Set 27** | vest, dust, kept, must, post, list, last, best, most, fast, just |
| **Set 28** | sweet, tea, been, asleep, sea, leaf, seat, read, seen, street |
| **Set 29** | rain, name, came, again, day, take, make, away, may, made |
| **Set 30** | pie, tie, nice, time, mice, night, bike, fly, try, by |
| **Set 31** | coat, boat, home, hope, rose, toes, coach, hose, goes, toe |
| **Set 32** | boot, school, too, soon, tooth, blue, room, new, grew, June |
| **Set 33** | an, as, can, can't, do, don't, is, isn't, be, because, him, night, or, so, want, said |
| **Set 34** | one, two, three, four, five, six, seven, eight, nine, ten |
| **Set 35** | look, book, cook, took, foot, wood, hood, cooking, stood, looking |
| **Set 36** | car, card, carpet, farmer, star, farm, shark, garden, sharp, market |
| **Set 37** | boy, toy, enjoy, annoy, royal, oil, coin, noisy, voice, noise |
| **Set 38** | owl, town, how, down, frown, crown, shower, flower, now, crowd |
| **Set 39** | mouse, house, out, about, shout, pound, mouth, count, loud, thousand |
| **Set 40** | Monday, Tuesday, Wednesday, Thursday, Friday, Saturday, Sunday, today, yesterday, holiday |
| **Set 41** | you, they, get, after, going, push, over, went, getting, are |
| **Set 42** | fair, hair, pair, air, repair, chair, stairs, fairy, there, where |
| **Set 43** | pear, bear, wear, their, tear, stare, scare, care, share, square |
| **Set 44** | fork, horse, born, sport, morning, forty, door, story, floor, poor |
| **Set 45** | saw, claw, yawn, dawn, autumn, sauce, paw, caught, taught, crawl |
| **Set 46** | core, snore, more, store, explore, sore, tore, bored, before, wore |
| **Set 47** | bigger, brother, her, were, over, under, sister, water, other, another |
| **Set 48** | bird, girl, first, third, circle, stir, dirty, thirty, thirsty, thirteen |
| **Set 49** | fur, curl, curve, purpose, nurse, burn, curtains, hurt, return, surprise |
| **Set 50** | ear, hear, near, clear, tear, beard, fear, disappear, appear, dear |
| **Set 51** | head, bread, instead, tread, spread, feather, heavy, weather, ready, steady |
| **Set 52** | eleven, twelve, thirteen, fourteen, fifteen, sixteen, seventeen, eighteen, nineteen, twenty |
| **Set 53** | red, orange, yellow, green, blue, purple, pink, brown, black, white |
| **Set 54** | laugh, little, some, went, come, called, with, could, should, have, would, here |
| **Set 55** | love, people, lived, many, who, live, much, very, our, than, your, once |
| **Set 56** | January, February, March, April, May, June, July, August, September, October, November, December |

# Our growing range of educational books:

**ENGLISH TODAY** — ISBN 1897737 02 5 — Price £2.99 Features grammar, comprehension and punctuation.

**SPELLING TODAY** — ISBN 1897737 01 7 — Each book in the Spelling Today series is priced at £2.99.
**SPELLING TODAY for ages 7-8** — ISBN 1897737 04 1 — These books have a unique design incorporating a flap which
**SPELLING TODAY for ages 8-9** — ISBN 1897737 09 2 — children can use to cover the words that they are learning.
**SPELLING TODAY for ages 9-10** — ISBN 1897737 14 9 — They write the words, then check them and write them again
**SPELLING TODAY for ages 10-11** — ISBN 1 897737 19 X — for valuable repeated practice.

**HANDWRITING TODAY Book 1** — ISBN 1897737 73 4 — Both handwriting workbooks are extremely popular, priced at
**HANDWRITING TODAY Book 2** — ISBN 1897737 78 5 — just £3.50 each.

**PINK PIG TURNS BROWN** — ISBN 1897737 77 7 — The charming story of a pig who gets dirty.

**MATHS TODAY for ages 6-7** — ISBN 1897737 28 9 — The Maths Today books each cost £2.99 and feature a wide
**MATHS TODAY for ages 8-9** — ISBN 1897737 33 5 — range of mathematical exercises. The number speed sections
**MATHS TODAY for ages 9-10** — ISBN 1897737 69 6 — provide excellent practice of mental arithmetic skills.
**MATHS TODAY for ages 10-11** — ISBN 1897737 38 6

**TIMES TABLES TODAY** — ISBN 1897737 00 9 — Price £1.99. Over **90,000** copies sold.

**MENTAL MATHS for ages 7-8** — ISBN 1897737 08 4 — Price £2.99. Very popular books, each providing repeated
**MENTAL MATHS for ages 8-9** — ISBN 1897737 13 0 — practice to help children to learn number facts. Removable
**MENTAL MATHS for ages 9-10** — ISBN 1897737 18 1 — answer section in each book.
**MENTAL MATHS for ages 10-11** — ISBN 1897737 23 8

**HOMEWORK TODAY for ages 9-10** — ISBN 1 897737 24 6 — Photocopiable resource books priced at £15.50 each. Fifty
**HOMEWORK TODAY for ages 10-11** — ISBN 1 897737 48 3 — homework activities in each book plus fifty answer pages.

**NUMERACY TODAY for ages 5-7** — ISBN 1 897737 53 X — £16.50 each. Very popular series of photocopiable resource
**NUMERACY TODAY for ages 7-9** — ISBN 1 897737 63 7 — books. More than sixty resource sheets together with sixty
**NUMERACY TODAY for ages 9-11** — ISBN 1 897737 58 0 — teachers' pages in each book.

**SPELLING FOR LITERACY for ages 5-7** — ISBN 1 897737 44 0 — £18.50 for 176 pages.

**SPELLING FOR LITERACY for ages 7-8** — ISBN 1 897737 49 1 — £16.50 for 128 pages in each book. Together with Spelling
**SPELLING FOR LITERACY for ages 8-9** — ISBN 1 897737 54 8 — for Literacy for ages 5-7, these books provide excellent
**SPELLING FOR LITERACY for ages 9-10** — ISBN 1 897737 59 9 — coverage of spelling throughout the primary age range.
**SPELLING FOR LITERACY for ages 10-11** — ISBN 1 897737 64 5

**BEST HANDWRITING for ages 7-11** — ISBN 1 897737 98 X — Transform the handwriting at Key Stage Two with this photocopiable resource book for teaching joined writing. Price £15.50.

All of our titles are available from W H Smith, Waterstone's, other leading retailers and independent bookshops. You may also like to visit our website: www.andrewbrodie.co.uk

For an up to date list of titles, just photocopy this form and post or fax it back to us.

Name: _____

Address: _____

_____

Postcode: _____ Telephone: _____

Email: _____

Andrew Brodie Publications ✔
PO Box 23 Wellington Somerset TA21 8YX
Phone/Fax: (01823) 665345
e-mail: orders@andrewbrodie.co.uk